Jun. 2, 2008

HIP-HOP

The United States exports products all over the world. One of its biggest imports is hip-hop. It has proved that music is indeed a universal language.

Hip-Hop Around the World

Ida Walker

Mason Crest Publishers

Hip-Hop Around the World

Produced by Harding House Publishing Service, Inc.
201 Harding Avenue, Vestal, NY 13850.

MASON CREST PUBLISHERS INC.
370 Reed Road
Broomall, Pennsylvania 19008
(866)MCP-BOOK (toll free)
www.masoncrest.com

Printed in the United States of America

First Printing

9 8 7 6 5 4 3 2 1

Library of Congress Cataloging-in-Publication Data

Walker, Ida.
  Hip-hop around the world / Ida Walker.
     p. cm. — (Hip-hop)
  Includes index.
  ISBN 978-1-4222-0293-7
  ISBN: 978-1-4222-0077-3 (series)
  1. Rap (Music)—History and criticism—Juvenile literature. I. Title.
  ML3531.W35 2008
  782.421649—dc22
                                    2007028093

Publisher's notes:
- All quotations in this book come from original sources and contain the spelling and grammatical inconsistencies of the original text.

- The Web sites mentioned in this book were active at the time of publication. The publisher is not responsible for Web sites that have changed their addresses or discontinued operation since the date of publication. The publisher will review and update the Web site addresses each time the book is reprinted.

DISCLAIMER: The following story has been thoroughly researched, and to the best of our knowledge, represents a true story. While every possible effort has been made to ensure accuracy, the publisher will not assume liability for damages caused by inaccuracies in the data, and makes no warranty on the accuracy of the information contained herein. This story has not been authorized nor endorsed by any of the artists mentioned.

Contents

Hip-Hop Time Line

1976 Grandmaster Flash and the Furious Five emerge as one of the first battlers and freestylers.

1984 The track "Roxanne Roxanne" sparks the first diss war.

1970s DJ Kool Herc pioneers the use of breaks, isolations, and repeats using two turntables.

1988 Hip-hop record sales reach 100 million annually.

1982 Afrika Bambaataa tours Europe in another hip-hop first.

1970s Grafitti artist Vic begins tagging on New York subways.

1980 Rapper Kurtis Blow sells a million records and makes the first nationwide TV appearance for a hip-hop artist.

1985 The film *Krush Groove*, about the rise of Def Jam Records, is released.

1970   1980

1970s The central elements of the hip-hop culture begin to emerge in the Bronx, New York City.

1983 Ice-T releases his first singles, marking the earliest examples of gangsta rap.

1986 Run DMC cover Aerosmith's "Walk this Way" and appear on the cover of *Rolling Stone*.

1979 "Rapper's Delight," by The Sugarhill Gang, goes gold.

1984 *Graffitti Rock*, the first hip-hop television program, premieres.

1974 Afrika Bambaataa organizes the Universal Zulu Nation.

1981 Grandmaster Flash and the Furious Five release *Adventures on the Wheels of Steel*.

1988 MTV premieres *Yo! MTV Raps*.

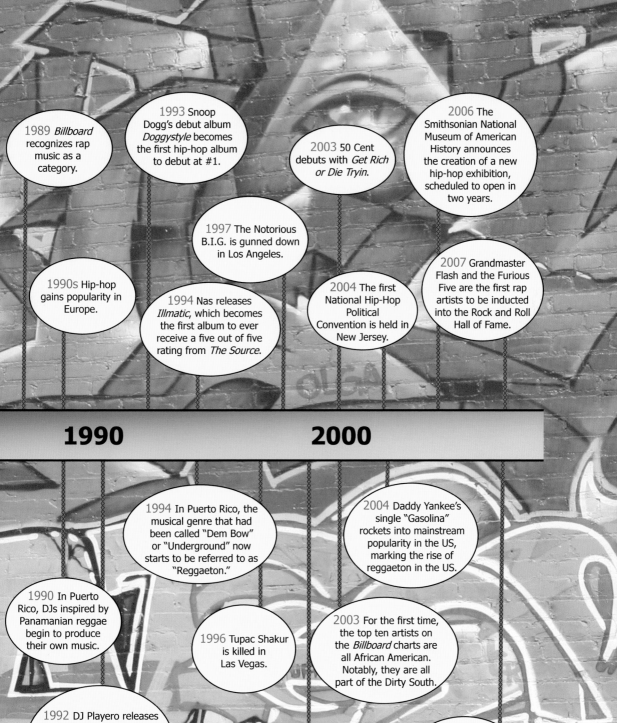

1989 *Billboard* recognizes rap music as a category.

1993 Snoop Dogg's debut album *Doggystyle* becomes the first hip-hop album to debut at #1.

2003 50 Cent debuts with *Get Rich or Die Tryin.*

2006 The Smithsonian National Museum of American History announces the creation of a new hip-hop exhibition, scheduled to open in two years.

1997 The Notorious B.I.G. is gunned down in Los Angeles.

1990s Hip-hop gains popularity in Europe.

1994 Nas releases *Illmatic,* which becomes the first album to ever receive a five out of five rating from *The Source.*

2004 The first National Hip-Hop Political Convention is held in New Jersey.

2007 Grandmaster Flash and the Furious Five are the first rap artists to be inducted into the Rock and Roll Hall of Fame.

1990

2000

1994 In Puerto Rico, the musical genre that had been called "Dem Bow" or "Underground" now starts to be referred to as "Reggaeton."

2004 Daddy Yankee's single "Gasolina" rockets into mainstream popularity in the US, marking the rise of reggaeton in the US.

1990 In Puerto Rico, DJs inspired by Panamanian reggae begin to produce their own music.

1996 Tupac Shakur is killed in Las Vegas.

2003 For the first time, the top ten artists on the *Billboard* charts are all African American. Notably, they are all part of the Dirty South.

1992 DJ Playero releases his mixtape *32,* which has some of the earliest examples of reggaeton recorded, including a track by Daddy Yankee.

2001 Russell Simmons founds the Hip-hop Action Network.

2007 Numerous hip-hop artists perform at the Live Earth concerts, which take place around the globe.

In 2007, Grandmaster Flash took a huge step on behalf of hip-hop and rap. That year, the Rock and Roll Hall of Fame opened its doors to one of the newest genres of music and welcomed Grandmaster Flash and the Furious Five as inductees.

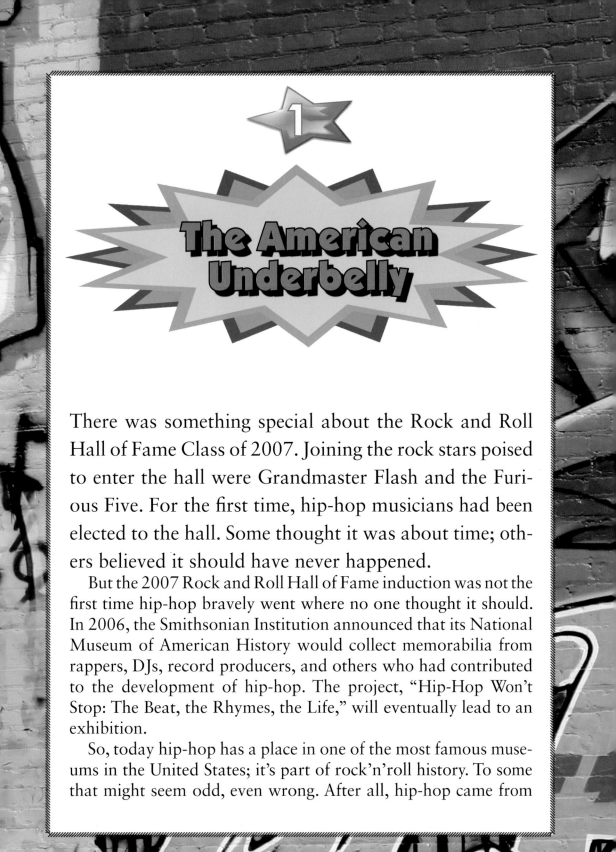

The American Underbelly

There was something special about the Rock and Roll Hall of Fame Class of 2007. Joining the rock stars poised to enter the hall were Grandmaster Flash and the Furious Five. For the first time, hip-hop musicians had been elected to the hall. Some thought it was about time; others believed it should have never happened.

But the 2007 Rock and Roll Hall of Fame induction was not the first time hip-hop bravely went where no one thought it should. In 2006, the Smithsonian Institution announced that its National Museum of American History would collect memorabilia from rappers, DJs, record producers, and others who had contributed to the development of hip-hop. The project, "Hip-Hop Won't Stop: The Beat, the Rhymes, the Life," will eventually lead to an exhibition.

So, today hip-hop has a place in one of the most famous museums in the United States; it's part of rock'n'roll history. To some that might seem odd, even wrong. After all, hip-hop came from what music pioneer Russell Simmons calls "the underbelly." It revealed the ugly side of American urban life; for some, its lyrics and rhythms were shocking, inappropriate, or downright offensive. Now, however, the Rock and Roll Hall of Fame cast its mantle of approval over hip-hop. Hip-hop had come a long way!

A Star Is Born

The culture that became hip-hop and the music that would become rap (though the terms are often used interchangeably) were born on the streets of the South Bronx, New York City, in the late 1960s and early 1970s. Money was scarce for many in the South Bronx, so people often made their own entertainment instead of going to clubs. **DJs** would hook up a sound system to the electricity that ran the streetlights. Then, while the DJs played their records, those in the neighborhood would gather on the street and in the parks to dance and have a good time.

One of the biggest names in the early days of hip-hop was Jamaica native Clive Campbell. Of course that wasn't a "cool" name for a DJ, so he became DJ Kool Herc. (Herc came from Hercules, a nickname Clive earned for his athletic skills.) Before long, everyone wanted Kool Herc to DJ their parties. He took the money he earned and created the loudest and baddest sound system he could. Everyone knew when Kool Herc was DJing!

During hip-hop's early days, the DJ was the main man (and DJs were men, not women) at any get-together. Those who came weren't there to listen to the music; they wanted to dance. It was the DJ's job to get the crowd up on the dance floor and keep them there. DJs kept the crowds moving by letting one record flow into another. There was no break between songs or dances.

A New Sound

The crowds who came to DJ Kool Herc's parties were mostly the black and Hispanic people who lived in his neighborhood. They weren't into the disco music popular uptown or even in other parts of the Bronx, so Herc adapted his playlist to fit the musical interests of his audience, adding funk to his stack. Funk music is a blend of *jazz*, the *blues*, and *soul*, a style popular with those who came to dance when DJ Kool Herc spun the disks.

But then Herc noticed something else. Whenever the vocals gave way to a segment that featured drums or other percussion instruments, the crowd ate it up. During these breaks,

When you're poor, going to clubs can be out of your price range. That's where the DJs came in during the 1970s in the Bronx. They would set up their turntables wherever possible, and a dance party soon followed.

the dancers *really* got into the rhythms. Now the trick was to find a way to expand the length of the breaks. In the book *The Vibe History of Hip Hop*, S. H. Fernando Jr. writes,

> *"Herc wondered what would happen if he got two copies of the same record and cut back and forth between them in order to prolong the break or sonic climax. Unwittingly, he had stumbled upon the break-beat."*

This technique was being used in Jamaica, but now DJ Kool Herc introduced it to the United States. Once again, he had hit on something his fans loved—and his creativity earned Herc the title of "godfather of hip-hop."

Some dancers really got into the rhythms provided by the extended breaks. During the breaks, these young men—called break boys or b-boys—would command the floor. The b-boys (and a few b-girls) moved their bodies in ways that seemed almost impossible (or at least extremely painful!). Eventually, the b-boys took their act to other parts of the city. During the 1970s and 1980s, people walking in New York City often happened on eye-popping demonstrations of the b-boys' skills.

Bam

But while all this artistic creativity was stewing, young people in the Bronx, especially those living in the black and Hispanic neighborhoods of the South Bronx, felt left out of **mainstream** society's opportunities. Poor schools, few jobs, and less money all contributed to the rise of drugs, gangs, and other illegal activities as outlets for urban youths' energy. Hip-hop, however, gave some young people a more constructive way to use their energy and spend their time.

Afrika Bambaataa, Bam, was one of those kids growing up on the streets of New York. He was a leader of the Black

Spades, one of the biggest street gangs in the Bronx. But he loved the music that came from the spinning turntables of DJ Kool Herc. In *The Vibe History of Hip Hop*, Bam describes what he thought after he first heard DJ Kool Herc:

> *"I liked what he was playing, it sounded funky, and I had all that . . . at home—all those records he was playing—so I said, once I come out and get my system, I'm gonna start playing that too."*

After his mother gave him two turntables for high school graduation, Bam was on his way. Before long, he had earned the nickname the "Master of Records." Two of early hip-hop's classics, "Big Beat" by Billy Squier and "Champ" by the Mohawks, were made popular at his shows.

Soon a rivalry developed between DJ Kool Herc and Afrika Bambaataa. But they didn't use guns to wage their war against each other, and they didn't use their fists either. Instead, they "fought" to see who could be the loudest, who could draw the biggest crowds, and who had the best breaks and b-boys. Everyone had fun. Hip-hop gave the streets new options: rapping and dancing instead of violence and drugs.

Grandmaster Flash and the Furious Five

Along about this time, a young man named Joseph Saddler was experimenting with electronic gadgets. He also loved music, and he created a way to hear on his headphones what was being played on one turntable while another was playing. Joseph's quick hands on the turntables earned him the nickname Grandmaster Flash.

Grandmaster Flash is credited with several innovations in hip-hop music, including scratching. Though the technique of scratching—purposely sliding the needle along the playing

One of the first major MCs was Grandmaster Flash. His quick hands earned him his nickname, and there was no question that he and the Furious Five put on a wild show whenever they performed.

record—was first discovered by Theodore Livingston, Grandmaster Flash was the one who made it an important part of the hip-hop sound. Some people might find the sound of the needle scratching the surface of the record annoying. Others might cringe at the thought of the record being ruined. But in the hands of Grandmaster Flash, scratching was an art form, creating even more danceable rhythms.

Grandmaster Flash was also at the forefront of a changing trend in hip-hop. In the beginning, the DJ was king. But things began to change when MCs became part of the performance. They spoke to the crowd, often in a call-and-response format, speaking (rapping) along with the rhythm of the song. The MCs gave people the chance to participate in the performance as well. Call-and-response was a part of African Americans' heritage, with a long history rooted deeper than slavery's dark days, way back in the culture of Africa itself. Churchgoing black Americans were already well acquainted with this technique of involving an entire crowd in a spoken performance— and now hip-hop turned call-and-response into a whole new game.

Most performances featured just one or two MCs, but Grandmaster Flash had five—the Furious Five: Cowboy, Melle Mel, Kid Creole, Scorpio, and Rahiem. They were so skilled that their individual voices blended into what seemed like only one voice. Through the wild success of Grandmaster Flash and the Furious Five and others, by 1978, MCs had taken over some of the star status that once belonged to DJs.

Getting the Sound Out There

Until the late 1970s, the only way you could hear hip-hop music was to go to a club or party or get a copy of a **bootleg** recording made during a performance. But in 1979 that changed with the release of "Rapper's Delight" by the Sugarhill Gang. Sylvia and Joe Robinson had formed the Sugar Hill record label and put together the Sugarhill Gang to get in on the hip-hop phenomenon. "Rapper's Delight" became the first hip-hop single to go *gold* and one of the first to hit the top-40 charts. Disco, which had been at the top of the charts for the past few years, was challenged by this new sound.

About the same time as "Rapper's Delight" was released, the Fatback Band released "King Tim III (Personality Jock)." Grandmaster Flash and the Furious Five, Afrika Bambaataa, and other hip-hop pioneers recorded with Sugar Hill and other new labels. Before long, traditional labels such as Mercury Records jumped onboard the hip-hop train with Kurtis Blow's "Christmas Rappin'." Hip-hop music became a mainstay on radio playlists. In 1986, Run-DMC's album *Raising Hell* was released. It became the first hip-hop album to achieve wide-spread popularity, and Run-DMC became the first hip-hop group to have its music played regularly on MTV.

Going West

By the 1980s, hip-hop found its way to the West Coast. The first nationally successful West Coast hip-hop song was Ice-T's "6n' Da Mornin'," released in 1986. The song is also considered to be the beginning of gangsta rap.

Gangsta rap features lyrics that talk about a lifestyle filled with sex, drugs, and violence. The first successful gangsta rap album, *Straight Outta Compton* by NWA (Niggaz With Attitude) was released in 1988. Besides being popular with black and white listeners alike, the violence expressed in the lyrics also caught the attention of the government. Some groups, including the FBI, tried to censor that album and other gangsta rap releases. Instead of turning off people to the sound, however, law enforcement's efforts made more people interested in the music.

The 1990s saw the rise of other West Coast gangsta rappers, including Dr. Dre, Tupac Shakur, and Notorious B.I.G. Unfortunately, the decade also saw the rise of hip-hop–related violence. Tupac and Notorious were both murdered in drive-by shootings, Tupac in 1996, and Notorious in 1997. Both murders are believed to have resulted from the intense rivalry between hip-hop artists on the West Coast.

Hip-Hop Criticisms

As hip-hop's popularity grew, so did the criticism surrounding the music. Most of the early hip-hop artists were male, and some critics pointed to the hateful and demeaning ways women were portrayed in many of the songs. Others criticized the violent lyrics of many songs.

But critics also pointed their fingers at the artists themselves. Shootings, drug busts, and beatings, although rare, made big news when they involved hip-hop artists. Some artists still draw criticism for their excessive lifestyles—too much bling, too many women, too fancy or too many cars, too many drugs. Others are criticized for what they say, such as Kanye West, when he spoke out against the way the aftermath of Hurricane Katrina was being handled. Kanye West was also criticized for his ego after his appearance as a Jesus-like character on a magazine cover. Others, however, praised Kanye for his courage.

Some of the criticism is justified, but much of it isn't, or at least it doesn't apply to all hip-hop artists. Violence and women hating, for instance, aren't characteristics of songs that will be released under LL Cool J's gospel rap label. And contrary to media stereotypes, hip-hop artists are often generous and willing to lend a hand to those in need.

In 1974, for example, Bam brought together a group of DJs, graffiti artists, and b-boys to create The Organization. Its purpose was to build social awareness through hip-hop. Eventually, the group's name was changed to the Universal Zulu Nation. The group organized neighborhood cleanups, food drives, and mentoring programs.

In 2001, music and fashion mogul Russell Simmons formed the Hip-Hop Summit Action Network (HSAN). HSAN has sponsored such activities as voter registration drives and leadership programs for youths. In 2007, Russell announced a drive to remove all questionable lyrics from radio versions of hip-hop songs.

Individually, hip-hop artists also make significant contributions to others. Many participated in benefits that followed the terrorist attacks on America and the hurricanes that struck the Gulf Coast. Ludacris and Kanye West have foundations that aid young people, especially through educational

Since its beginnings, hip-hop has been the music of the streets—the tales of the real world. Some might say that Kanye West has been "too real." The outspoken star has been criticized for his opinions, and for perhaps thinking too highly of himself.

and recreational programs. The Peapod Foundation, formed by the Black Eyed Peas, helps people in Africa. Clearly, people should be careful not to judge the entire hip-hop culture by the actions of a few.

Hip-Hop Today

In 2007, hip-hop remains a force on the music scene. Women have become strong voices in the music, though they are still the minority. From Salt-N-Pepper, the first major successful female group, their numbers have grown to include Lil Kim, Destiny's Child, Fergie, Queen Latifah, and Ciara. Even musicians who aren't really known as hip-hop artists, such as Madonna and Alicia Keys, have recorded hip-hop songs. Hip-hop has also made it into mainstream culture. Its songs are featured in films, television shows, and commercials.

Hip-hop was never just about the music, however. Graffiti artists were part of the hip-hop culture since the beginning, and they still *tag* almost anything that doesn't move. In some cities, the artwork is celebrated as a major part of the area's culture. Fashion hasn't been immune to hip-hop's influence either, and it's not just young people who have adopted the fashion trend!

Perhaps more significant, hip-hop is no longer just an American phenomenon. Today it has spread all over the world. And even before hip-hop sprang to life in the Bronx, its early roots were already growing in another part of the world.

In geographic size, Jamaica is a small country; but in its influence on music, the island nation is one of the biggest. Though the United States is credited as the birthplace of hip-hop, the movement owes much of its history to Jamaica.

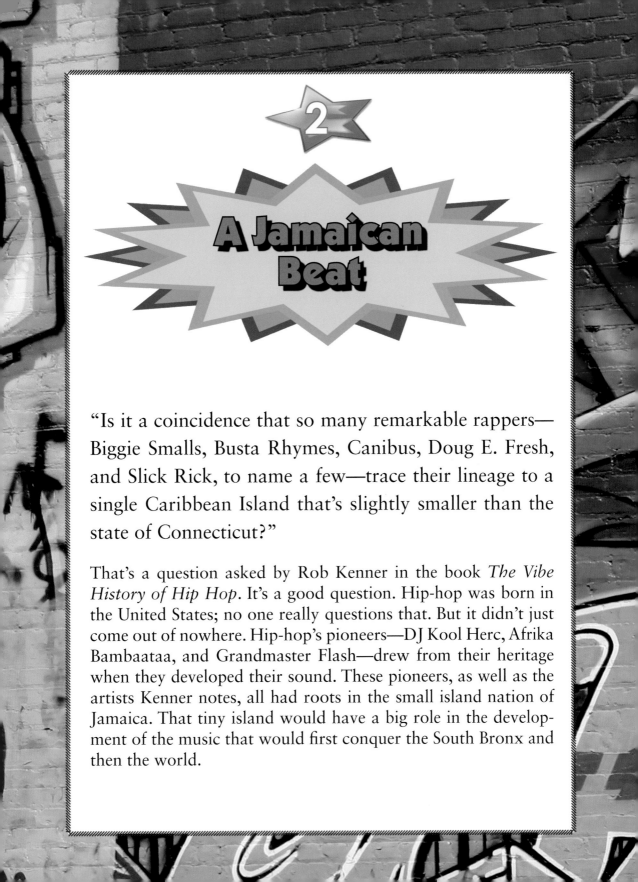

2

A Jamaican Beat

"Is it a coincidence that so many remarkable rappers— Biggie Smalls, Busta Rhymes, Canibus, Doug E. Fresh, and Slick Rick, to name a few—trace their lineage to a single Caribbean Island that's slightly smaller than the state of Connecticut?"

That's a question asked by Rob Kenner in the book *The Vibe History of Hip Hop*. It's a good question. Hip-hop was born in the United States; no one really questions that. But it didn't just come out of nowhere. Hip-hop's pioneers—DJ Kool Herc, Afrika Bambaataa, and Grandmaster Flash—drew from their heritage when they developed their sound. These pioneers, as well as the artists Kenner notes, all had roots in the small island nation of Jamaica. That tiny island would have a big role in the development of the music that would first conquer the South Bronx and then the world.

The Birth of Reggae

Much of Jamaica's population lives in extreme poverty. Most have little hope of ever breaking out of the cycle that keeps families poor for generations. Without money to buy expensive toys or fancy nights out, many people turn to simple pleasures—dancing and music. In the 1960s, mobile discos traveled throughout Jamaica, giving people a chance to listen to music, dance, and forget about their troubles for a while.

Reggae grew out of that desire to have fun, but it became so much more. Behind the creation of reggae was Clement "Sir Coxsone" Dodd, one of the biggest names in Jamaican music. His portable disco kept many Jamaicans entertained with records he had gone to the United States to get.

According to legend, Sir Coxsone wanted to create an original sound. Traveling to the United States to get the latest records had become too time-consuming, so he and some associates got together to create ska, a fast music with heavy emphasis on rhythm. A few years later, musicians took elements of Jamaica's native ska, calypso, and traditional African music, and fused them with America's rock and soul, which were very popular on the island. The sound that came out of the experiment featured heavy beats and was slower than ska. They called it rocksteady.

Rocksteady was not destined for a long life; by 1968, most musicians had moved on to something new. What came out of their next musical experiments was faster than rocksteady and more complex than ska. It was reggae.

Bob Marley

One of the best-known reggae artists is Bob Marley. Along with the Wailers, Bob brought reggae off the island. Before long, it was popular in the United States and in Europe. Through the sounds of Bob Marley and the Wailers, the world learned about Jamaica.

Perhaps most important, Bob Marley and many in his group were Rastafarians, a religion that honors Haile Selassie, a former emperor of Ethiopia, and stresses black culture and identity. Social justice is also important in their belief system, and Bob took that responsibility seriously. Listeners heard songs that spoke about poverty, injustice, and other social ills. The songs told of life as the listeners knew it—just as hip-hop would do a few years later.

One of the biggest influences on hip-hop was Jamaica's reggae music. Like hip-hop, this was the music of the people. It was a way for those living in poverty to tell their stories. It was also a way for the same people—and many others—to put aside their problems for a while and have fun dancing.

U-Roy

The development of Jamaican music didn't stop with reggae. Around 1980, a new genre evolved from reggae, dancehall. Dancehall was faster than reggae, and some of the lyrics were a bit questionable in taste. Many performers began to use drum machines instead of drum sets. Perhaps one of the most important differences was toasting.

Toasting was the practice of rapping, talking, or even singing over rhythm patterns. One of the best-known "toasters" was a Jamaican welder named Ewart Beckford. Onstage he was called U-Roy, and he poured a flood of energy into the rhymes he spewed over the mic. It was his responsibility to work the crowd up into a dancing frenzy. U-Roy did that, and he did it well. When Jamaica native DJ Kool Herc looked for inspiration as a DJ, he turned to U-Roy and other toasters, such as Dennis Alcapone.

Reggaeton

Just as reggae evolved from earlier music *genres*, it in turn led to the emergence of new forms of music. The most popular and most successful is reggaeton.

Unlike reggae, reggaeton did not begin in Jamaica. Its birthplace is the Central American country of Panama, though Puerto Rico also played a big role in its development. According to some music historians, reggae came to Panama with Jamaicans who came there to find work. By the 1990s, Panama musicians were creating their own reggae sounds. Throughout the 1990s, the music evolved in both Panama and Puerto Rico, drawing influences from dancehall and hip-hop as well as reggae. As with its predecessors, rhythm is vital to reggaeton. In reggaeton, the basic rhythm is called "Dem Bow," a title taken from a song by Jamaican dancehall artist Shabba Ranks that features a strong drum machine track.

Though most of the best-known reggaeton artists sing, the lyrics are usually rapped or performed by a combination of rapping and singing. Just like hip-hop, the songs often tell of life's problems. But they also talk about more pleasant things, such as partying and dancing.

Another characteristic reggaeton shares with hip-hop is gender: most of the reggaeton artists who have found success are male. Two of the biggest names in the genre are Daddy Yankee and Don Omar, who have found incredible success in the United States and around the world. Although women got a late start in reggaeton, more female performers, such as Ivy Queen, Glory, and K-Mil, are joining its ranks.

Full Circle

Jamaica and its music, including reggae and dancehall, had a major influence on the development of hip-hop. Many of the leaders of early hip-hop had ties to the small nation, and they looked to the island for inspiration. As a result, a small island has played a big role in music all over the world.

Jamaican music, like hip-hop, has close ties to Africa. Slavery's cruelty could never silence the rhythms of the long-ago homeland across the Atlantic. Ironically, hip-hop's deepest roots were in Africa's soil—and now, its branches stretched full circle, back to Africa, where modern-day Africans discovered hip-hop.

Music has been important in African culture for centuries. When hip-hop came to the continent, its rhythm and movement were a natural fit with many of Africa's cultural traditions. As it grew in popularity, the young people of Africa put their own stamp on it.

Hip-Hop in Africa

From the beginning, rappers looked to the world around them—the violence, the poverty, the drug scene—for inspiration. This is a characteristic hip-hop follows wherever it goes, and it is true today for urban youth in Africa. South Africa and Tanzania have been especially successful in creating their own brand of hip-hop.

Hip-Hop Comes to South Africa

America's hip-hop craze hit the African continent in the early 1980s. Young people in Africa loved the dancing, the use of percussion, and the graffiti art that were major parts of American hip-hop, and they adapted them to fit their lives. One of the first African hip-hop groups was Black Noise, from Cape Town, South Africa. The members of Black Noise began as graffiti artists, spreading their messages around the city and country, and eventually became well known in the area as b-boys. In the late 1980s, Black Noise also earned a reputation as MCs.

Black Noise became as well known as possible in the South Africa of the 1980s, but being a hip-hop artist in the 1980s was difficult—even illegal—in that country because of apartheid. Under this government policy, individuals were classified by color groups; the major classifications were white, black, colored, and Asian. Each group was kept separate from the

Much of the early history of hip-hop in South Africa will remain a mystery for a long time—perhaps forever. Out of fear that it could bring discontent to the population, the government made hip-hop illegal until the repeal of apartheid. The identities of the country's hip-hop pioneers are often unknown.

others, and nonwhites had little if any voice in how they were governed. For many nonwhites, especially the black population, life was very difficult. Many spent their lives mired in extreme poverty and unsanitary conditions. It was a life from which few could see any escape.

When South African musicians began adopting the hip-hop culture as their own, the government got worried. Government officials could see what was happening with hip-hop in the United States, where performers were rapping about violence, injustice, poverty. The South African government was afraid if it let hip-hop loose in their country, the same thing would happen. And they weren't far off the mark. Performers and graffiti artists used their music and art to speak out against apartheid, calling for freedom for all people. To stem the civil unrest the government feared was on its way, it outlawed hip-hop.

It didn't work. The government might have been able to slow the growth of the music and cultural movement, but hip-hop had too much people power behind it to be stopped completely. In 1993, with the end of the apartheid policy at last, the South African government lifted the restrictions on hip-hop. Now people could listen to rap on the radio, and television stations had permission to show rap videos on the air.

Kwaito

Hip-hop has played a significant role in the development of the music genre Kwaito. Though some people call it South Africa's hip-hop, that's not completely accurate, and not fair to either form of music.

Kwaito is a blend of hip-hop, South African jazz, and township pop. Some performers rap the words, and others chant or even shout the lyrics. Though the performance style might differ, hip-hop and Kwaito do share some characteristics.

According to the documentary *South Africa's Kwaito Generation* (www.insideout.org):

> *"Like American hip hop, kwaito was built from the ground up, originating in what its performers often refer to as 'the ghetto.' (In this case, though, that ghetto is in Soweto, the township where blacks were forced to live during apartheid)."*

Like hip-hop in the United States, some in South Africa saw Kwaito as a way out of poverty. The documentary goes on to say:

> *"The music has afforded young blacks opportunities they could only have dreamt of under forced segregation. It has meant financial freedom for some. Moreover, it has given them the chance to exercise their recently won freedom of speech; to address the new struggles (AIDS, crime, xenophobia) that have developed in the wake of the struggle; and to bring their experiences to the TVs and radios of a nation that is still discovering its identity."*

In other words, like many of the hip-hop artists in America, Kwaito stars see the music form as a way to spread a message—and make money in the process.

Because hip-hop's and Kwaito's beginnings occurred while the genre was illegal in South Africa, the names of many of its South African pioneers many never be known. Some of today's performers, however, are making names for themselves in South Africa and beyond.

Jits

Jitsvinger, or Jits (born Quinton Goliath), is one of the biggest hip-hop stars in the country. Two of the country's most successful music producers—Grenville Williams and Ej Von Lyrik, better known as High Voltage—produced his hit album *Skeletsleutel*. Jits has been nominated for numerous music awards and is a frequent guest on television shows that feature the hottest hip-hop artists. He has worked with a German hip-hop group, Each One Teach One, and has lent his talent to a Swiss-South African **collaborative** album for the Rogue State of Mind project. Proceeds from that album's sales go to a charity in Cape Town.

Jits' skills aren't limited to music; he is also an award-winning poet. He frequently reads his poetry on television and has participated at the prestigious Spier Poetry Festival. Jits has also worked as a writing tutor with the Robben Island Museum Summer School off the coast of South Africa.

KONFAB

Another African hip-hop artist began his career at a young age. One 1992 night, eleven-year-old Sneez snuck out of his home in Maseru, Lesotho. His father punished him severely when he found out where Sneez had gone—the Palace Hotel, a strip club more than eighteen miles from home. Sneez didn't go there to watch the show or listen to the music, though. Instead, he and his crew, By All Means, *were* the music.

Even at eleven, it was clear that Sneez was meant for a career in hip-hop. Hip-hop was popular in Maseru, and a young boy could easily get caught up in the idea of being a star. But Sneez wasn't just dreaming; he was talented. Backed by some of his friends, he entered a hip-hop competition and won.

In 1999, Sneez moved to Cape Town, where he began to gain an audience. He eventually decided that people weren't going to take his childhood nickname Sneez seriously, so he began using the name KONFAB. No matter what you call him, KONFAB has made a major impact on the South African hip-hop scene. His lyrics are confrontational, anti-establishment, and just the kind of thing the South African government worried about during the days of apartheid. During much of the time KONFAB was writing about defying "the man," though, he was working a regular nine-to-five job as a civil engineer. According to KONFAB, this prepared him to write about such things more honestly.

Swart Gevaar, KONFAB's first album, was released in the summer of 2007. The songs are partly based on his personal experiences while working on a construction site in Wellington. Although apartheid is now history, KONFAB found that old habits die hard, and his experience on the construction site continued to find its way into his lyrics.

Young Nations

One of the most successful South African hip-hop artists doesn't even live in that country. Young Nations, a South African of Zulu heritage, grew up in South Central Los Angeles, California. His father had been forced from South Africa because of the stand he took against the government during apartheid. Growing up in Los Angeles, Young Nations became actively involved in many organizations focused on empowering youth all over the world. He helped organize the largest protest against apartheid in Los Angeles, and he was one the youngest members of Children of War, a nonprofit organization of young refugees from war-torn countries around the world.

In 1989, Young Nations traveled to South Africa. While there, he lived in Guguletu Township. That experience influenced his work when he returned to Los Angeles in 1991. In 1994, he released his first album, *K.A.S.H.*, which stood for Kept in Africa's Subliminal Hold. The album quickly caught the attention of the music world in California. He opened for such big names as Ice Cube, Coolio, and the Lynch Mob.

In June 2003, Young Nations' music found its way onto the South African music scene with his song "Win." "Live My Life," his follow-up, told about life growing up in South

Africa's segregated black communities. Another song, "Mr. Hustla," has been described as "pure b-boy hip-hop at its absolute finest."

Tanzania and Bongo Flava

On the east coast of Africa is Tanzania, home to one of the fastest growing music genres in the world—Bongo Flava. Like South Africa's Kwaito, Bongo Flava was heavily influenced by American hip-hop.

One of the biggest names in African hip-hop is Young Nations, though he grew up in Los Angeles. As a young star, he had the chance to tour with such huge hip-hop performers as Ice Cube and Coolio (shown here).

Hip-hop began to exert an influence on Tanzanian music in the late 1980s. Almost from the beginning, it was extremely popular. As Tanzania's musicians, MCs, and dancers took up hip-hop, they modeled their acts on what had come from the United States. One of the first crews was the Kwanza Unit, and other early hip-hop groups included Mr. II, the Hard Blasters, and Gangwe Mobb.

Music wasn't the only thing the early Tanzanian hip-hop artists adapted from American rappers. They also took on the

In Tanzania, the Maasai, such as the singers shown in this photo, have had a major influence on hip-hop. Their traditional style of chanting is often combined with rapping.

look of the American stars, following their lead in fashion and attitude.

As Tanzanian performers became more familiar and comfortable with hip-hop style, they made it their own. They took some of their local dance music styles, such as muziki wa dansi and Indian filmi, and mixed them with the techniques of American hip-hop and even some rhythm and blues, soul, swing, and *salsa*. Bongo Flava is the result of this musical mixture.

Bongo is the nickname of Tanzania's largest city, Dar es Salaam, where most of the Bongo Flava performers live and work. It is also the Kiswahili word for brain, *ubongo*. The "flava" refers to the flavor these individuals give to the area through their music.

Like American hip-hop and the Kwaito of South Africa, Bongo Flava songs deal with many of the issues faced by its performers and audiences. Songs are performed in Swahili, with an occasional English word or phrase thrown in, and they deal with AIDS, poverty, success, and money. These are subjects to which young people all over the world can relate; these topics have shaped the international language of hip-hop and its successors.

Unlike the censorship hip-hop artists encountered in South Africa, performers in Tanzania and other countries along the east coast of Africa have had a relatively easy time getting their music heard. Television and radio programs often showcase the talents of local hip-hop and Bongo Flava artists. However, Bongo Flava is still little known outside Tanzania.

Tanzanian Hip-Hop Musicians

Despite the fact that Tanzanian Bongo Flava has been slow to expand beyond the border, there have been a few musicians who have gained a wider audience. One such group is X Plastaz from Arusha, a town in northern Tanzania. The group consists of three brothers, their teenage brother and sister, and

Hip-hop has spread throughout the continent of Africa. What started as an American import has evolved to become Africa's. Each country or region has added its own ingredients to make the music relevant to its people.

a Maasai singer. The group combines Maasai chants with rapping in Swahili and Haya. The group's *Maasai Hip-Hop* has been a huge success in the region.

Another major group on the Tanzanian music scene is Wagosi wa Kaya, which means "homeboys" in Sambaa. The group's fame quickly spread throughout Tanzania. Their fans appreciated the fact that they rapped about issues that were important to them—health care, education, police corruption. The regional commissioner in Tanga, Wagosi wa Kaya's home region, banned their song "Tanga Kunani" ("What's Going On in Tanga") because it hit a little too close to home. He believed the song's lyrics reflected badly on the region.

Elsewhere in Africa

Other parts of Africa also enjoyed their own forms of hip-hop. Three of the most popular hip-hop groups in Nigeria are SWAT ROOT, the Trybsmen, and the Plantashun Boyz. The most influential hip-hop magazine in Africa, *African Beatz*, is also published in Nigeria. The style arrived a little later in Kenya, but once it got there, young Kenyans couldn't get enough of hip-hop. Kalamashaka, 2 Kenyans, and Gidi Gidi/Maji Maji are just three of the groups making a name for themselves in the genre.

All over Africa, musicians have embraced hip-hop, enjoying the American version of the genre and making their own uniquely African styles. Meanwhile, in other parts of the world, other hip-hop artists are doing the same thing: finding music that they like and making it their own. Even the straight-laced British are joining in, rhyming and rapping to hip-hop's rhythms.

When hip-hop went to Great Britain, the United States had its chance to get even for the 1960s' British Invasion. Britain was already a big fan of "different" when it came to music and fashion (it is the birthplace of punk after all), and its music fans lapped up the American export.

Hip-Hop in Great Britain

In the 1960s, Great Britain invaded the United States. This *British Invasion* had no guns or cannons, just some guys with long hair, guitars, drums, keyboards, and talent. Almost thirty years later, the United States got even, invading Great Britain with hip-hop.

The Early Years

Like young people in the United States, those in Great Britain were enthusiastic about this new music and cultural form called hip-hop. British youth joined their American counterparts tagging buildings, boxcars, and anything else that stood still long enough. They adopted the fashions worn by rappers and hip-hoppers in American cities. B-boys could be found making their moves in many clubs in Great Britain.

Just as had happened in New York, British rappers did not rush to lay their sound down on record tracks. Instead, they concentrated on performing live, feeding on the energy of the crowd gathered for one purpose—to dance. An occasional bootleg tape would make its way from one fan's hands into another's, but the emphasis was on the live performance. Meanwhile, some pop groups, such as Adam and the Ants and Wham, added some rap elements to their more traditional sound.

By the mid-1980s, British record companies wanted to take advantage of this hot new trend, since there was no evidence that hip-hop's popularity would end anytime soon. British sales of records by American rappers were huge, and the record companies wanted to cash in on that business. The wildly successful British Invasion and Beatlemania had proved that British musicians could find success in America, and British record companies saw no reason why that success would not repeat itself.

Great Britain Rap Goes to Disk

Some of the earliest British rap artists copied the American style; a few English performers even used American accents during their performances. In time, though, the British artists gained self-confidence and developed their own style and used their own accent.

In 1983, Britain had its first homegrown rap record: the single "London Bridge Is Falling Down" by the DJ Newtrament, released by Jive Records. Newtrament didn't make any other recordings, and "London Bridge" achieved only small success, but that didn't stop other record companies. They didn't want to rush in, though; they released albums and singles slowly, teasing rap fans and allowing hip-hop's popularity to develop.

As popular as hip-hop was in Great Britain during the 1980s and 1990s, it faced a major problem: most radio stations wouldn't play the records or even publicize the performances. If you're trying to make it in the music world, that's not a good thing. Pirate radio stations that played rap popped up frequently, but just as frequently they folded. To publicize releases and concerts, performers and record companies often depended on word-of-mouth advertisement. That might be a good way to spread gossip, but it was an unreliable way to persuade people to buy recordings.

Hip-hop artists and their record companies were not without their champions, however. Radio DJs Dave Pearce, Tim Westwood, and John Peel encouraged their stations to play rap, and hip-hop began to get airplay on some of the major radio stations in Great Britain. With radio play and the creation

When the Beatles (shown in this photo) came on the scene, American teens couldn't snap up their latest offerings quickly enough. When hip-hop arrived in Britain, teens in the UK were anxious to buy the latest. In what seemed like a smart move, record companies decided that homegrown rappers would be a huge hit. They were wrong.

of hip-hop record labels, releases came more frequently. "London Bridge Is Falling Down" was followed by *Street Sounds Electro UK* (1984), featuring MC Kermit; "Kids Rap/Party Rap" (1985) by the Rapologists; and "Don't Be Flash" by DJ Richie Rich (1985).

The first British hip-hop artist to find chart success was Derek B. His success was followed by that of Hijack, the Demon Boyz, Hardnoise (who later became Son of Noise), and MC Duke. The success of those musicians encouraged the development of a more British rap sound. Jazz and reggae influenced some groups, including Outlaw Posse and London Posse, respectively. Wee Papa Girl Rappers became one of the first female hip-hop groups in Great Britain, and developed a pop-based form of rap that radio stations were more likely to carry on their playlists.

But despite the success of these groups, the hip-hop market in Great Britain was still small. Once it became obvious to the artists that sales, chart position, and radio play were necessary to be successful, a conflict developed among some of the artists. Some, such as Gunshot and Son of Noise, felt that those who charted were sellouts. To them, Derek B and Rebel MC, who had songs on the chart, had forgotten the "edge" that had given original hip-hop its voice.

A New Millennium, a New Generation

Most British hip-hop artists chose to ignore the possibility of being labeled a sellout. During the early 1990s, several hip-hop legends came to the forefront, including Massive Attack, Blade, Overlord X, and Krispy.

Unfortunately, the success that British hip-hop experienced in the 1990s didn't last. The record companies never had sales that matched—or even came close to—those of American artists. The British fans were more likely to buy albums put out by Americans than by their own rappers. Meanwhile, Americans bought hardly any British hip-hop albums. Paying for the right to **sample** sections from the songs of one artist on another artist's recordings proved to be too much for several record companies. Most had to drop artists from their labels, and for many, the costs eventually meant they had to close their doors.

British hip-hop didn't end, though it just changed. Hip-hop became more pop oriented. As the new millennium approached, kids who had grown up on hip-hop were now the ones making the music. The new artists had names like Mark B, DJ Skitz, and Roots Manuva. In 2002, BBC1Xtra, a radio station featuring black music, went on the air. Along with digital radio, the station's programs were available online, and hip-hop now had a better way to hook up with its fans.

A new form of British music, Brithop, has emerged with the new century, and its success has increased every year. A **fusion** of urban and hip-hop music, Brithop has seen success with artists such as Sway and Rok-Wila. Though hip-hop's success in Great Britain might fall far short of American rap, it's far from a dead genre.

Derek B

Unlike hip-hop artists in the United States, the names of most of those in Great Britain are still unknown to audiences outside the country. The first artist to chart a hip-hop song was Derek Boland, better known as Derek B. Growing up, Derek was a big fan of the British band The Who; America's Queen of Soul, Aretha Franklin; and Jamaican reggae star Bob Marley.

Derek began his music career as a DJ, touring clubs in London when he was just fifteen. Later, he worked for some of the pirate radio stations that sprang up during hip-hop's early years. Eventually, he began his own station, but he was bored and went to work for a record label. He decided to record his own a track, "Rock the Beat," and took the name Derek B. Two more of his albums hit the charts, and he was one of the first rappers to appear on *Top of the Pops*, a British music television program.

Overlord X

Overlord X—Benjamin Balogun—began his hip-hop career as a teenager when he took some turns as a DJ. When he was fourteen, he began rapping, and a star was born.

In 1988, Overlord X released his breakthrough single, "14 Days in May." The song was a testimony against capital punishment, telling the story of Edward Earl Johnson, who had been executed based on a confession he claimed he was forced to give. Overlord X then released a series of very successful albums before leaving his label because of creative differences.

Next, he managed a boy band called Benz, using the name Tim Shade. When the band folded in 2000, Overlord X moved on to running his own production company, Mo-Am Masters, while continuing to work as an artist.

Roots Manuva

Roots Manuva, born Rodney Smith, made his record debut in 1994 with the group IQ Procedure. Two years later, he released his first solo single, "Next Type of Motion." In 1998, Roots released his first solo album, *Brand New Second Hand*. His experiences growing up as the child of Jamaican immigrants inspired him; the album's title refers to the fact that because money was scarce, Roots often received used items for gifts.

The album was a hit, and Roots' place in British hip-hop was set. A reporter for the *London Times* wrote:

> *"his is the voice of urban Britain, encompassing dub, . . . and hip hop as it sweeps from crumbling street corners to ganja-filled dancehalls, setting gritty narratives against all manner of warped beats."*

One of the few British hip-hop artists to make it big is Roots Manuva. Like many of the genre's pioneers, he can trace his roots to the island of Jamaica.

A reporter calls Roots "the voice of an urban Britain." As hip-hop artists have done throughout its history, Roots uses music to tell the story of the real world of Britain—especially as experienced by those living in poverty.

The *Times* wasn't the only one impressed with Roots' work. Later that year, he received a MOBO (Music of Black Origin) award as Best Hip Hop Act.

Today, Roots continues to record with his own label and also develops new talent for the British hip-hop scene.

Hip-Hop on the Move

Hip-hop's rhythms have proved irresistible to urban youth around the world. When American hip-hop spread across the Atlantic Ocean, it did not stop at Great Britain. All of Europe, and indeed the world, has been influenced in some way by hip-hop music and culture.

Hip-hop has hit on a common thread throughout the world—telling the story of how things really are for people who might be living on the fringes. The genre has spread throughout Europe.

Hip-Hop in Europe—and Beyond

By the late 1970s and early 1980s, hip-hop had developed a fan base in the United States. It wasn't on solid footing yet, but it was popular enough that some of the biggest names in hip-hop began working on expanding the genre beyond the U.S. borders. Their first stop was France.

Hip-Hop in France

Hip-hop first appeared on the French music scene in the late 1970s, not long after it found success in the United States. In 1982, the legendary Afrika Bambaataa, Fab 5 Freddy, and the Rock Steady Crew were part of the New York City Rap Tour, the first hip-hop concert in France. Afrika had a big influence on the fledgling French hip-hop movement, and it wasn't just about the music. French hip-hop star MC Solaar had the opportunity to see Afrika; years later, he told *Newsday*:

> **"Bambaataa provided rap with a philosophical basis—peace, unity, positivity—which was tremendously appealing to the French. He also told us to rap in our native tongue and to reflect local reality."**

Though the tour moved on, it left behind break-dancing teenagers and **underground** rap concerts, as well as the idea that people could use hip-hop for more than entertainment. Hip-hop could be a force for social change.

The first French hip-hop record was *Paname City Rappin'* by Dee Nasty. But the 1984 release was just the beginning. Before long, it seemed as though French hip-hop fans couldn't get enough. Hip-hop radio stations sprang up in France, but unlike the pirate stations in Great Britain, they lasted.

France's hip-hop artists are often from the poorer regions of Paris and other major cities. Among the artists who found popularity in France were Assassin, Lunatic, and Zebda. Some, like Saian Supa Crew, received some popularity outside of France. But by far, the best-known rapper from France is MC Solaar.

Born Claude M'Barali in Senegal, a country on the west coast of Africa, MC Solaar's family moved to a Paris suburb while he was still a baby. When Claude was twelve, he moved to Egypt to live with his uncle for eight months. There he learned about Zulu Nation and Afrika Bambaataa. When he returned to Paris, Claude concentrated on music. He took the stage name MC Solaar while still a teenager, from his graffiti tag Soar.

In 1990, MC Solaar moved to Paris to pursue a music career. It didn't take long for the young star to find success. His first album, 1991's *Qui Sème le Vent Recolte le Tempo* (He Who Sows the Wind Reaps the Rhythm), became the first rap album to be certified **platinum** in France. He quickly became the first French hip-hop star to become popular outside France as well, even developing a following in America. His North American fan base increased in 2004 when his song "Le Belle et Le Bad Boy" was featured on the last episode of the hit television series *Sex and the City*.

Music experts point to MC Solaar's lyrics as one of the reasons for his international success. Instead of focusing on violence and women hating, as some American rap artists do, he uses poetic wordplay to get across his message. Although he doesn't shy away from the important issues of the day, he delivers the message with more subdued language.

Hip-Hop in Italy

Hip-hop found its way to Italy in the early 1990s, later than in many other countries. Early Italian hip-hop was influenced by ragamuffin music, which came to the country from Jamaica at about the same time as rap. American hip-hop had a major influence as well, of course, though in an article in the *International Herald Tribune*, one manager of a rap group is quoted as saying, "Rappers are much nicer here."

Besides rapping in Italian, some artists use local dialects, language specific to a particular area. When *Billboard* asked Lupo of the group Nuovi Brigati of Sicily why they did so, since it limited the number of people who could understand them, he responded,

> *"We did our own cultural research . . . and one reason we chose dialect is because we don't want it to die . . . and we have a lot of things to say, particularly coming from the South, with its problems of Mafia, corruption, and unemployment."*

Regardless of language, Italian hip-hop follows the trend of rapping about issues important to the audience.

Articolo 31 of Milan was one of the first Italian hip-hop groups to grab the attention of the country's mainstream music audience. At first, the group styled itself after the rap popular in New York City. Then, despite some initial success, the group evolved its sound into one that was oriented more toward punk and pop.

The first real star of Italian hip-hop was Jovanotti (Lorenzo Cherubini). His music was primarily pop oriented, with some hip-hop elements thrown in. He did release a few rap disks,

In Greece, hip-hop coexists alongside some of the world's oldest ruins. The walls of the Acropolis, shown in this photograph, must have heard a far different kind of music back in the classical days of ancient Greece!

including a cover of the Sugarhill Gang's "Rapper's Delight." Frankie Hi-NRG MC (Francesco Di Gesù) has been compared to Nas, but his lyrics are less obscene. For example, he uses soccer metaphors in his song "Rap Lament" to describe the inefficiency of the Italian government.

Music isn't the only part of hip-hop that has been adopted in Italy. The country is a fashion haven, with Milan one of the capitals of high-fashion design. Many young people have tossed aside the tailored look of mainstream Italian dress. Instead, according to Daniel Marcoccia of *Groove* magazine, they prefer more casual, "sloppy" American styles. "There's a lot of interest in fashion," Marcoccia says. "Rappers love to show their brands. Hip-hop is tied to gadgets."

Hip-Hop in Greece

In Greece, hip-hop is tapping out its modern rhythms in the midst of an ancient landscape that includes the Parthenon, Mount Olympus, the Acropolis, and the first Olympic Games. Italian hip-hop can be traced back to 1987, but it really didn't get a foothold until the mid-1990s, when the first Greek-language albums were released.

From its earliest days, competition between performers in Greece was intense. Active Member was one of the most important groups in Greek hip-hop, and as other groups formed, such as the Living Dead, Active Member became the target of rumors, gossip, and dissing by the new groups. Active Member continued to be an important force in Greek hip-hop, however, while the Living Dead basically self-destructed. Not only did the Living Dead feud with other hip-hop artists, the group argued within itself. They could only keep things together long enough to record one album.

Greek hip-hop followed the path set by American artists. As some American hip-hop lyrics became more violent and demeaning to women, so did the words of Greek rap. Eventually, songs about guns, violence, sex, and drugs became common-place.

When rap first came to Greece, many critics shrugged it off as a passing fad—just one more American thing that would come, be popular for a while, and then vanish. Instead, in the years that have passed, rap's popularity has only gotten hotter. Imiskoumbria and Terror X Crew are often credited as being responsible for bringing rap into the Greek mainstream. They were the first Greek groups to have albums certified gold, a major accomplishment in any country.

Hip-Hop in Serbia

Even in Serbia, formerly part of Yugoslavia, hip-hop is popular. When hip-hop came to Europe in the early 1980s, break dancing and rap quickly caught on with Serbian young people. The Master Scratch Band released the first Serbian rap recording in 1984. Musicians like Budweiser, Green Kool Posse, and Robin Hood soon followed. Gru released the country's first major album in 1995, and Serbian hip-hop continued to grow until the Kosovo War broke out in 1999.

The war was expensive, and the country's economy took a severe hit. Some groups were dropped by their labels, and few new rappers were being signed. But just a few years later, things started to turn around. By 2002, a new label was formed and rap was back.

Hip-Hop Circles the Globe

North America, Africa, and Europe are not the only continents pounding with hip-hop's relentless rhythms. Hip-hop has spread to many cultures and lands around the world.

For example, the Maori, New Zealand's native population, have used rap to express their support for self-rule. Hip-hop artists like the Wanderers and Temple Jones became heroes among the Maori. Eventually, the Maori and other Pacific Islanders developed their own style of rap, Urban Pasifika, which fuses American-style hip-hop with Maori language rhymes and Pacific Island instruments like the ukulele. Che Fu and Scribe are among the best-known Urban Pasifika artists.

China, Jordan, and Israel also have small but growing hip-hop cultures, despite political and religious objections in those countries. In 2007, the European Union even sponsored a hip-hop dance workshop in Amman, Jordan.

Despite the controversy hip-hop has experienced in the United States and around the world, it continues to thrive, giving those without power a chance to express their opinions, to make a difference, to be relevant. That's a desire everybody understands, no matter their language or culture.

So it's no wonder hip-hop has traveled so far from its earliest beginnings in the South Bronx. By the twenty-first century, it has become a truly global voice for independence and creativity. For many minority cultures around the world, hip-hop is a powerful tool for solidarity and self-respect. It is a voice that has the strength to speak out against injustice—and it's loud enough to be heard by almost everyone!

1960s	The British Invasion hits the United States.
late 1960s	Hip-hop is born in the South Bronx.
1968	Reggae develops in Jamaica.
late 1970s	Hip-hop finds its way to France.
1973	DJ Kool Herc gets his first DJing gig, and a legend is born.
1974	Afrika Bambaataa forms The Organization, which will later be renamed the Universal Zulu Nation.
1978	MCs take over from the DJs as stars of hip-hop.
1979	"Rapper's Delight" is released and becomes the first hip-hop single to go gold and reach the top-40.
1980s	Hip-hop comes to Africa.
1980	Dancehall becomes popular in Jamaica.
1982	The New York City Rap Tour plays France.
1983	Britain has its first homegrown rap record, DJ Newtrament's "London Bridge Is Falling Down."
1984	*Paname City Rappin'*, by Dee Nasty, becomes the first French hip-hop record.
1984	The Master Scratch Band releases the first Serbian rap recording.

1986 Run DMC's *Raising Hell* becomes the first hip-hop album to achieve widespread popularity.

1986 "6n' Da Mornin'" becomes the first nationally successful West Coast hip-hop song.

1987 Hip-hop appears in Greece.

1988 *Straight Outta Compton*, by NWA, becomes the first successful gangsta rap album.

early 1990s Hip-hop comes to Italy.

1990s The popularity of gangsta rap soars.

1990s Reggaeton develops, first in Panama and then spreading to Puerto Rico and other Latin countries.

1991 *Qui Sème le Vent Recolte le Tempo*, by MC Solaar, becomes the first rap album to be certified platinum in France.

1993 The South African government lifts its ban on hip-hop music.

1994 Young Nations releases *K.A.S.H.*, and he becomes a big hit in California.

1995 Gru releases Serbia's first major rap album.

1996 Rapper Tupac Shakur is murdered in a drive-by shooting.

1997 Notorious B.I.G. is murdered in a drive-by shooting.

1999 The Kosovo War breaks out, curbing the growth of hip-hop in Serbia.

2001 Music and fashion mogul Russell Simmons forms the Hip-Hop Summit Action Network (HSAN).

2006 Smithsonian Institution's National Museum of American History announces the Hip-Hop Won't Stop: The Beat, the Rhymes, the Life project.

2007 Grandmaster Flash and the Furious Five are inducted into the Rock and Roll Hall of Fame, the first hip-hop artists to be so honored.

2007 Russell Simmons proposes that all questionable language be removed from rap recordings intended for radio airplay.

2007 The European Union sponsors a hip-hop dancing workshop in Amman, Jordan.

Books

Bogdanov, Vladimir, Chris Woodstra, Steven Thomas Erlewine, and John Bush (eds.). *All Music Guide to Hip-Hop: The Definitive Guide to Rap and Hip-Hop*. San Francisco, Calif.: Backbeat Books, 2003.

Chang, Jeff. *Can't Stop Won't Stop: A History of the Hip-Hop Generation*. New York: Picador, 2005.

George, Nelson. *Hip Hop America*. New York: Penguin, 2005.

Kallen, Stuart A. *The History of Latin Music*. Farmington Hills, Mich.: Thomson Gale, 2006.

Kusek, Dave, and Gerd Leonhard. *The Future of Music: Manifesto for the Digital Music Revolution*. Boston, Mass.: Berkley Press, 2005.

Light, Alan (ed.). *The Vibe History of Hip Hop*. New York: Three Rivers Press, 1999.

Waters, Rosa. *Hip-Hop: A Short History*. Broomall, Pa.: Mason Crest, 2007.

Watkins, S. Craig. *Hip Hop Matters: Politics, Pop Culture, and the Struggle for the Soul of a Movement*. Boston, Mass.: Beacon Press, 2006.

Web Sites

Foundation of African Hiphop Culture Online
www.africanhiphop.com

H2Ed
www.h2ed.net

Hip-Hop Association
www.hiphopassociation.org

Hip-Hop Summit Action Network (HSAN)
www.hsan.org

National Hip-Hop Political Convention
www.hiphopconvention.org

Glossary

blues—A music style that developed from African American folk songs in the early twentieth century, and that consists primarily of sad songs.

bootleg—An illegally made product.

British Invasion—The popularity and influence of British rock groups in the United States, starting with the Beatles and the Rolling Stones during the 1960s.

collaborative—Achieved by working with others on a project.

cut—To manually queue up duplicate copies of the same record in order to repeatedly play the same passage.

diva—An extremely arrogant and glamorous woman, especially an actress or singer.

DJs—Disk jockeys; those who play recorded music for the entertainment of others.

fusion—The blending of musical styles or elements from more than one tradition.

genre—A category into which artistic works can be placed based on form, style, or subject matter.

gold—A designation that a recording has sold 500,000 units.

jazz—Popular music that originated among black people of New Orleans in the late nineteenth century, characterized by syncopated rhythms and improvisation.

mainstream—The ideas, actions, and values that are most widely accepted by a group or society.

platinum—A designation indicating that a recording has sold 1 million units.

salsa—A type of Latin American dance music combining elements of jazz and rock with rhythmic African-Cuban melodies.

sample—A piece of recorded sound or musical phrase taken from an existing recording.

soul—A style of African American music with a strong emotional quality, related to gospel and rhythm and blues.

tag—a signature or identifying symbol used by a graffiti artist.

underground—Outside of the prevailing and established social or artistic environment.

Index

About the Author

Ida Walker is the author of many nonfiction books for teens and young adults. She lives in New York, where she is a full-time author and editor.

Picture Credits

Flickr/cc-att-sa 2.0-jimmyrog: p. 23
Garces, Juan / PR Photos: pp. 8, 26, 32, 48, 54
Hatcher, Chris / PR Photos: p. 24
iStockphoto: pp. 18, 40, 45, 53
    Hood, Eric: p. 12
    Klusacek, Milan: p. 31
    Murat: p. 21
    Nehring, Nancy: p. 42
    Oanta, Flavius: p. 51
    Tzolov, Nick: p. 11
    Zivana, Ufuk: p. 16
Kirkland, Dean / PR Photos: p. 2

Front cover collage: iStockphoto, Nicholas Monu, Doug Schneider, Alexandr Tovstenko

To the best knowledge of the publisher, all other images are in the public domain. If any image has been inadvertently uncredited, please notify Harding House Publishing Service, Vestal, New York 13850, so that rectification can be made for future printings.